Angel Karma Strikes Again

In Indian lore the Heyoka had permission to enter any secret society or meeting and behave anyway they wanted, even 'mooning' people. Their role was to keep people from taking themselves too seriously. They could make fun of everything and everyone, many times at their own expense. Self-sabotage is part of the Heyoka/Coyote's art and with the electric charge of constant creation he has no conscience. The unconscious will is his guide, for he is totally without ego.

I invite you to celebrate your Coyote Medicine and enjoy the freedom of being willing to look foolish as you practice the Spiritual Warrior's greatest challenge – letting go of self-importance.

Pam Drinnon

© 2013 by Pam Drinnon.

All rights reserved. No part of this book may be reproduced, stored in a retrieval system, or transmitted by any means, electronic, mechanical, photocopying, recording, or otherwise, except under contract with the publisher.

Published by

IAMPress
3053 Dumbarton Rd.
Memphis, TN 38128

Acknowledgements

I want to thank all the people who played in my "Script" and helped me create funny stories to tell. I am truly grateful to my wonderful late sister LaVern, my chief-editor and co-writer, and Wendy Daniels, my beloved daughter, a professional writer whose standards pushed me to write better and to not give up my dream. Final editing was by Ashley Drinnon, my granddaughter. Without their loving support and encouragement this book would never have happened. May you enjoy reading these stories as much as I enjoyed writing them.

I want to thank Jim Powell and Cecil McDaniel with IAMPress for their coaching, layout and design work. Anne Enoch and Andrew Walker contributed to the illustrations.

Coyote Angel Pam

"The ultimate result of shielding men from the effects of folly is to fill the world with fools." Herbert Spencer

Table of Contents

INTRODUCTION	v
FIRST IMPRESSIONS	1
A SECOND CHANCE	4
MY GREEN HAIR STORY	8
A HAIRY SITUATION	15
CAREFUL WHAT YOU ASK FOR	20
THE FACE FAIRY	25
HOT WAX STORY	29
THE MANICURIST	33
SOMETHING FOR NOTHING	37
SPRAY TANNING	42
SNOBELLE'S BIRD	47
A BROW WAX FOR CHRISTMAS	53
EDSEL'S EYEBROWS	58
THE BRAZILIAN	65
LAUGHING COYOTE STORY	71
Looking for Hair Therapy	75
The Italian Stallion	79
Too Natural For Me	84
A Shaky Situation	89
About the Author	94

INTRODUCTION

Pam and I were born and raised in the beauty business. Our Aunt Trinna opened the first beauty salon in Kingsport, Tennessee. Our Mom married our Dad in 1934 when she was just fifteen. She apprenticed as a beautician with Aunt Trinna. Several of our aunts and cousins also apprenticed or worked for Trinna so it was only natural for Pam and me to follow in their footsteps. In time Pam would open the first unisex hair salon in Collierville, Tennessee!

This is a collection of humorous stories based on Pam's adventures through her years in the beauty business. We referred to them as Angel Karma stories - since we believe we are "angels in disguise" working with each other on our karma through the law of attraction. The law is simple – what you give, you receive back three-fold.

These stories are meant to entertain *and* remind us that it's okay to laugh at ourselves. It could be said that the Laughing Buddha is the truest representation of enlightenment in that He is always looking for the "cosmic joke" - for He understands that the joke is on us!
Many Blessings,

LaVern McKarem, a.k.a. Chief Uppa Creek

Pam Drinnon, a.k.a. Coyote Angel

Chapter One

FIRST IMPRESSIONS

I always do my best to make a great first impression with each new client. I know I must be prepared for whatever shows up. Every client has specific needs (or desires) and you must be ready to fulfill them to the best of your ability. It's easy to lax and feel as if you've seen it all, then in the blink of an eye a twist of fate blows the whole thing up in your face.

I'm totally focused as I lean over my client's face, carefully applying the wax below her eyebrows. My hand trembles slightly - what's wrong with me? I've done so many of these, why am I nervous? I place a small strip on the eyelid and quickly pull it off.

I stare in disbelief – the middle part of her eyebrow is missing! How did this happen?!

Unbelievable! I'm in shock. My first thought is how I can try to explain this.
My second thought – perhaps I can dye the skin to match. No, she'll wonder what I'm doing and why it's taking so long. My third thought? Maybe I'll pencil it in and she won't see it till she cleanses her face in the evening. No, that's not very angel-like.

I realized at this point that the entire situation was a set up from the beginning. I knew all too well that we attract that which we fear the most, and Amy came to me plenty worried after a string of bad experiences at other salons.

The moment she reclined in my chair she started complaining about her last waxing and the botched up job the hairdresser had done. She had also gotten her hair permed – or fried, as she described it – that same day and now her hair was breaking off at the scalp. She informed me she had been growing out her eyebrows so they "could be done right." Sure, no pressure. I assured her that eyebrows were my forte and not to worry. I would do them correctly.

She remained fearful, and so created yet another beauty shop blow-up!

What could I do? Vow that I would never work on a complaining client again? Once more, someone's fear placed me directly in the role of the bad guy. With karma it's a dirty job, but somebody's gotta do it.

Spiritual teachings dictate that what we continuously think or say gives us more of it. If you say "I want this, I want that…" you are creating a constant state of want! Spirit says yes to what we ask and so we create unconsciously. As for myself, I wish I would be conscious enough to not get caught in this scenario ever again! There I go, saying what I don't want. If only it were so easy!

Chapter Two

A SECOND CHANCE

When you work with the public it never ceases to be challenging at times. If you don't mind the occasional heart-racing situation, then the beauty business is for you! It seems that just when you think you have something down pat, you love the work, and your confidence is flying high, a challenge walks through the door. BAM! The universe humbles you and sets you back to wondering if you will ever get it right!

We as humans live under the illusion that our ears are evenly spaced on our head. One thing I quickly learned was that they most certainly are not! That is why my least favorite salon service is ear piercing. I cringe when someone wants this service - ouch!

It was Donna's first visit to the spa, and she needed another piercing in one earlobe. After wearing heavy earrings for years her left ear lobe had been pulled down so far that it made it impossible to wear earrings. All she could wear were clip-ons, and they looked crooked all the time. Since her business was designing jewelry she was completely self-conscious at the strange looks she received from her customers. She even started tilting her head so her earrings would look balanced! Oh, the vanity of humans.

It was already a bad day for piercing, as my last client had been a 5 year old (yes, her mother's idea) and had screamed at the top of her lungs the entire time, totally traumatizing everyone involved. So I was nervous when trying to match up Donna's ear holes. I would eye her face very carefully, but every time I marked her earlobe it was too high or too low. After 15 minutes of this I finally let her mark it. I wasn't taking any chances - if it wasn't perfect it was her call.

With utmost care I slid the ear-piercing gun in place, just to see the earring stud fall out of the gun. Now I had to stop and replace it, then re-sterilize everything. Now I was really getting nervous. By the time I placed the piercing gun back on her ear the location mark had smudged! Oh well, here goes anyway... POP!

Donna grabbed her ear and yelped, "Oh God, I forgot how much this smarts!"

As I removed the gun I could see the piercing wasn't high enough. ARRGH! Tears stung Donna's eyes as she looked in the mirror and saw it wasn't right.

I apologized profusely and asked her to let it heal then come back in a week to try again. She was not happy at all and I silently prayed she would go someplace else. After she left I screamed, "That's it! No more ear piercing! Let someone else do it!"

But of course, guess who shows up the following week when I am the only one available? So be it. This time I was not going to become nervous. I calmly took her into my room and set up the gun. I placed a dot on her ear and pulled the trigger. POP! This time God was with me and it was perfect – I didn't even close my eyes this time! (Just kidding.)

Why she had to do that piercing twice I don't know. Perhaps her "angel karma" caught up with her!

Chapter Three

MY GREEN HAIR STORY

The harder the life lesson the bigger the laugh. When the laugh is on you, though, it doesn't seem that funny at all. But as time passes whenever the memory of the embarrassing event floats through our thoughts, we start to grin, then giggle at the entire situation. Seeing it in a new light allows us to laugh at ourselves – and realize we are hilarious!

There are some experiences in life that one would like to forget, but my sister and daughter kept asking me to write my 'Green Hair Story'. This happened so many years ago you'd think they would give it a rest, but they insisted until I relented.

In 1975, after moving to Memphis from Kingsport, in east Tennessee, I found work in a small salon. A year later I opened my own salon in Collierville, just outside of Memphis. I felt extremely lucky that most of my clients followed me.

However, when Calvin and his wife Mona showed up one day, I was really surprised; I never thought Mona would follow me as she was not an easy person to please. She was always complaining that her hair was never "perfect" enough; if she waited longer than 3 minutes past her appointment then you were given a lecture on the importance of her time; and she constantly grumbled about the cost of our services and often pushed for free extra treatments. To say I wasn't thrilled to see her was an understatement.

Calvin, on the other hand, was a gem. He was the opposite of Mona - laid back and easy to please. He was a funny man who loved to tell jokes, and when he was in my chair he kept me laughing. Calvin had lost most of his hair when he was in his 30's. "Male-pattern-baldness," he said, "It's hereditary."

Because of this he wore a hairpiece for several years until the hair that was left on his head started turning grey and his ash-blonde toupee no longer matched. Mona made fun of him so he hadn't worn it in years. I'm certain Calvin missed it though, because every time he sat in my chair he mentioned it, and finally asked me if it was possible to color his natural hair to match the toupee. It seemed like an easy thing to do but I had only been out of Beauty School for three years and was <u>way</u> over confident in my ability to color hair.

My sister LaVern worked with me at the salon. She had been a hairdresser for years and was once a beauty school instructor. I knew she could help me out if anything happened. She grumbled that my confidence over-reached my knowledge, and made it clear that she would brain me if I kept attempting to correct someone's hair color without consulting her first. I paid little attention to her fussing and knew I could always call on her expertise.

I asked Calvin to bring his toupee the next time he needed a haircut and I would see what I could do. He returned several weeks later with the 'rug' in hand.
"What's that?" I asked.
"My hair piece!" he beamed.

To be honest it looked more like road kill! This would definitely be a challenge. I carried his toupee to the stock room to see if I could find a color that would make his real hair match.

Voilá! I found the perfect color. I applied it to Calvin's hair and had him sit back at the shampoo sink for the color to process and finished cutting another client's hair in the meantime. Gray hair is generally resistant to color, so I decided to leave it on the full thirty minutes before checking it.

The shop was filled and people were waiting in the reception area when Calvin's wife, Mona, showed up and talked LaVern into squeezing her in for a haircut. I suspected she really wanted to see how Calvin's hair was turning out. I don't think she wanted him to start wearing his toupee again.

Thank heavens LaVern is cutting her hair, I thought, or Mona would be hanging over me and being a real pain. Her nature was picky and demanding, with a temper to match. You didn't want to get on her bad side! I felt sorry for Calvin because he was such an easy-going guy and she was his exact opposite.

When Calvin's timer went off, I took a wet towel and wiped a section of hair to check the color - it was <u>*bright green*</u>! I quickly washed his hair, hoping it would help. But the color didn't change - it was still green, *grass* green - he practically glowed!

Now I wished I had talked this over with LaVern. I could hear her scolding me, "Just because the color on the bottle looks like what you need, doesn't mean it will come out the same color, or be even close when applied on certain hair." I had promised to consult her before diving in to someone's hair color again. I couldn't ask for her help because I didn't want Calvin's wife to find out. I glanced up to make sure Mona was still in LaVern's chair then threw a towel over Calvin's head so he couldn't see his hair and start freaking out.

"Be right back Calvin," I said, and headed for the supply room to look for some red hair color to negate the green. LaVern said if hair ever turned green, applying red color straight from the bottle would usually cancel it out. Of course we had every color but red! I couldn't believe it. Ordering supplies was my job so I had no one to blame but myself.

If only Mona wasn't there I could explain to Calvin what happened and tell him not to worry, that I could fix it. But I did not want to get into it with Mona. I checked Calvin's hair again - it was still green as grass. I had to get some red color, fast! I told Calvin I wanted to apply a conditioner to his hair, and would he mind lying back in the sink while it was on.

"No problem, it feels good lying here. I might take a nap," he said.

After putting on the conditioner I draped a towel over his hair, grabbed my purse, and flew out the front door to my car. Walgreen's was across the street, and I drove there in one minute. They had plenty of red hair color, but I wasn't sure if I needed a dark or a light red, or maybe strawberry blonde. I couldn't decide. I needed help. Dang it!

Using the cashier's phone (this was before cell phones) I quickly called the shop. Thank heaven LaVern answered the phone.

"LaVern," I said, "what's the best shade of red to take the green out of hair?"

After a period of confused silence I heard, "Pam?! Where are you?" LaVern thought I was still in the shop and was looking around for me.

"I'm at Walgreen's. The color I put on Calvin's hair turned green, and we're out of red color - that's why I'm at Walgreen's. I need to buy some red hair color to get the green out!" Again, there was silence on the line. I could picture her eyes rolling.

"Vernie, I know you're working on Mona. Don't let on that you're talking to me and for goodness sakes, keep her in your chair and don't let her see Calvin's hair. I have a conditioner and towel on his head. You've got to look at his hair and tell me what shade of red to buy!"

"Hold on," she said in exasperation. In a minute she was back on the phone. "You weren't kidding about his hair!" she whispered in the receiver. "Get the reddest red you can find, and hurry back here! I don't know how long I can keep Mona occupied. She keeps craning her neck towards the shampoo bowl to see why Calvin's still lying there."

I picked a color called 'Reddest Fire Red' and quickly returned to the shop. If this didn't work, nothing would. I managed to sneak back in the shop and ran to the stock room to prepare the color. I didn't want Calvin to know I was applying more color to his hair, so I opted not to wear rubber gloves lest I give myself away (my hands were stained red for days). I kept working the color into his hair, and finally after ten long minutes the green faded away. Well, mostly faded. A greenish tinge was barely noticeable.

I set Calvin up, grabbed his toupee, slapped it on his head, and directed him to my station. I fussed and trimmed on his real hair and the toupee until it almost blended together. Close enough! He was happy and kept looking at Mona, who sat with her arms crossed and a frown on her face. I thought she was going to be angry, but instead she said it looked okay, better than she remembered.

After they left, LaVern and the other two stylists burst out laughing. By then they were all aware of what was going on. I was left completely drained from the ordeal and wanted to vent about it but all LaVern could do was laugh and laugh. It wasn't that funny to me! It made me want to give up coloring hair forever. It's like having a baby. As soon as the ordeal is over you swear you will never do it again. But the memory fades until we find ourselves facing it again!

Chapter Four

A HAIRY SITUATION

If you look at the hair color section in any drug store you would think that anybody could do it. Products today make it look easy for first timers, and there are plenty of colors to choose from. Just pick one you like, then read and follow the directions - simple, no? No! By taking your life - I mean hair - in your own hands and coloring it yourself, you might create a nightmare. If you must, find something that's not permanent. Correcting a bad "dye job" can cost much more than having it done professionally in the first place!

I don't know why hair stylists do not like do-it-yourself hair color. I have profited many times from the disasters that ensue. One example was Bobby Ray, a long-time client who called to see if I had time to dye his graying mustache. He had a date with a new honey and wanted to look as young as he felt. Unfortunately I was booked solid, but I could do it the following day. I could hear in his voice that he was disappointed. I promised to call him if someone cancelled.

At 10 o'clock that night my phone rang. "Pam, honey, it's Bobby Ray. Can you remove color from a mustache?"

Alarm bells went off in my head, "Oh no, Bobby, what have you done?"

He explained that after watching me put color on his hair so many times he thought it would be easy. So he went to the local drug store and bought some color for mustaches only. He told me how he read the directions and had no problem applying the concoction, but while waiting for it to process he got on the phone with a friend and forgot about the time. The instructions were specific – leave on for five minutes. He left it on for thirty.

Bobby Ray had a light gray, brownish mustache. This did not sound good.

"Did it turn real dark?" I asked and held my breath. "Hon, it's black! You've gotta help me!" "Bobby Ray, you idiot, why didn't you let me do it?!"

"Now I knew you'd be mad, but ain't there something I can do tonight? I can't stand to look at myself! Every time I pass a mirror I jump because I don't recognize myself. It scares me! I think there's a burglar in the house!"

Despite my best efforts I could not contain my laughter at the thought.

"I've already washed it 17 times - three times with Comet and my tire brush. Now it has a green cast!"

"Don't panic, Bobby," I advised him as I forced myself to stop laughing. "Just leave it alone and come to the shop first thing in the morning. I'll try to get the dye out."

He arrived bright and early all right, but came in to the salon with his head down and a big band-aide on his upper lip. "Now what have you done!" I cried in alarm.

I removed the band-aide. Above his lip was a black stain and one less mustache. "Bobby Ray what happened? Didn't I tell you to leave it alone?"

"Now Hon, I know, I know," he placated me with that slow drawl of his, "after we talked I couldn't stand looking at it. I drank a couple of six packs and decided to trim it. I was really getting into all the different ways to style it, but the more I whittled on it the more I laughed, and try as I might I couldn't get it to come out even! I just kept cutting it smaller and smaller until it looked like David Niven's (an actor from the 40's) who had just a thin line of hair across the lip, Then I saw this really dark shadow in its place and knew there was no way to salvage it."

By now Bobby Ray had me laughing so hard I was doubled over. "Well," I managed to say as I wiped the tears from my eyes, "what can I do now that you've shaved it off?"

"It ain't so much about how I look without a mustache, but can you get some of this dye off my skin? Besides having this huge space between my lip and nose, I also have a permanent 5 o'clock shadow! I look like a freak!"

Chuckling, I took him to the shampoo bowl and told him to relax while I found my lash and eyebrow tint remover. Each time I applied the solution to his skin he yelped and winced. Yeah, I know it stung, but it was the safest product I had to use on his face and I knew it would work.

He left the salon with a red, tender upper lip and some wisdom gained – for painful lessons tend to be lessons well learned.

"Got a full six pack, but lacks the plastic thing to hold it all together." Quote taken from actual (U.S.) Federal Employee performance evaluations

Chapter Five

CAREFUL WHAT YOU ASK FOR

It's hard to get motivated to go to the gym. Why not buy your own treadmill and use it at home? Even I have considered purchasing one. Lord knows I need the exercise. Well a friend of mine did just that. He purchased the Cadillac of treadmills with dozens of different speeds and all the bells and whistles. He's owned it for less than a year and now says he hates it. Why? Because he feels guilty for not using it in spite of the fact that he's still making payments on it!

There is much truth in the adage "Be careful what you ask for - you just might get it." I have no doubt we get what we ask for, which often ends up being what we believe we *deserve*.

A case in point involved my best friend Annie. One afternoon she and I sat down to Mastermind (a powerful prayer method where we evoke our good), and when it was her turn to ask for something she wanted, she said a treadmill. Each morning she asked "Little Annie" (her referral to her sub-conscious mind) to help her find a treadmill to exercise on. "It doesn't have to be new," she said. "I don't want to be greedy."

"This is great!" I thought. Annie had been talking about wanting to loose weight for some time.

For years I had been sharing information with Annie about the power of the sub-conscious mind and the law of attraction, (The sub-conscious mind is totally goal oriented.) and how to use the sub-conscious mind to manifest what we desire. I knew Annie was a powerful creator - and if she set her intention, she would get what she wanted. I told her to get a clear picture in her mind because the sub-conscious works best with pictures, or better yet, put a picture of a Treadmill on her refrigerator. "Every time you look at it, picture your self on it," I told her. "Any time you think of the treadmill, affirm, "I am worthy of all good things and my desires are always met."

A few evenings later, I got a call from Annie. It worked! She was getting a treadmill! "And the best part is that it's free!" she said excitedly. She went on to explain how right after she arrived home, Myra - her next-door neighbor - came over to ask if she knew anyone who might want a treadmill. She had seen her neighbor put his treadmill out on the curb and it looked to be in pretty good shape.

"Wow, this is unbelievable! This is really big! It's only been two days since we Masterminded! I love how this creating stuff works. I didn't even have time to put a picture up on my fridge. I just kept seeing myself working out on my treadmill. You've got to come over and see it!"

I arrived just as her husband Jeff got home. Annie couldn't wait to tell him about her great find and would he retrieve it for her. He rolled his eyes, "Okay Annie, just remember it may be broken." But we were caught up in Annie's enthusiasm, and so we followed her out to the curb and carried the treadmill back to their living room. After examining and testing it Jeff discovered it had a small problem; it only worked on high speed.

"Oh I'm sure you can fix it!" Annie said. Jeff wasn't completely sure he could. Annie would need to order a part, but he might be able to repair it.

In a couple of days the part arrived and Jeff installed it. I came over to see how the treadmill project was coming along. Annie was beaming. I asked her if they had tried it out. "No, we've been waiting for the new part, but I think it's time to give it a try."

Annie asked Jeff to show her how it worked, and with rapped attention we watched Jeff climb on the treadmill, flip the switch, and off he ran. He made it look easy, but as a postman he also walked every day on the job.

Suddenly, their seven-year-old son Alex wanted to try. Alex the invincible jumped on, hit the switch, and was instantly flung through the air into the other room. He was stunned, but otherwise unharmed.

We laughed so hard our sides hurt. Finally, it was Annie's turn. She stepped on the treadmill, put a death grip on the handle, ducked her head down and yelled to Jeff, "Hit the switch!"

The next thing she knew she was running for dear life and screaming, "Turn it off! Turn it off!"

Jeff switched it off and Annie fell to the floor. I laughed so hard my face hurt, every time we tried to stop one of us would start snickering and we were laughing again.

Annie got exactly what she asked for. "It doesn't have to be new," I chided her. "I don't want to be greedy." It seems that we are the ones who truly limit ourselves. We don't believe ourselves worthy of opulence and abundance – the First Class treatment. We reduce our expectations as protection from being disappointed.

Dream big but be specific, and remember that it's okay to go First Class.

Chapter Six

THE FACE FAIRY

Most people want to do things perfectly - no one really wants to make dumb mistakes. However, we are human and inevitably do the best we can at any given moment. When things start going south, I know my ego (pride) has got in the way. The day this incident happened I was feeling full of myself. In order to convince the salon to try a new, expensive skin care line, I promised it would be easy to sell and practically fly off the shelves. The pressure was on to jump start the sales and I wanted everyone in the salon to experience it – and they certainly did!

Oh boy! The new skin care line finally arrived at the shop. I snatched up a box of the under-eye gel roll-on pens I ordered. They were perfect to carry for an instant touch up to smooth lines under the eyes. I open it up, and gently rolled it below my eye. It felt cool and had a nice tightening effect on my skin. Wow! This is great, a roll on tube that I can carry with me and apply anytime needed. No more crinkly eye lines - fun!

I rounded the corner and spied Roe, one of my favorite hairdressers. She asked me what I was smiling about.

"This new product for the under eyes," I said. "It works great! You wanna try it?"
"Sure! I'll be your guinea pig."

I gently rolled the gel under Roe's eyes - she immediately started batting her eyelids. "Wow, Pam, that's strong!"

I then turned to Courtney, our massage therapist, and Julie, the receptionist, to see if they would like to try it. They both said yes, so I rolled the gel under their eyes.

Roe was still in discomfort. "Pam, is this suppose to make your eyes water?"
"No", I replied.

"Well, I must be sensitive to it - my eyes are stinging and they won't stop watering!"

I looked over at Courtney and Julie and they were blinking their eyes too. Perhaps I applied too much.

"Honey, go blot some of it off," I said. They all three headed for the restroom.

Tina, our hair tech, was shampooing a client and saw me applying the gel and said, "What's our Face Fairy up to today? Is that some of the new skin care line?"

"Yes," I said, "let me put some on you. Lean over here." This time I put a dab on my finger and pat it under her eyes. "The other girls thought it was too strong."

Michele, another hair stylist, was watching us, and asked what I had. I explained to her and her client how this eye gel pen was great for lines, puffy eyes and dark circles, and had a great tightening effect. Her client said, "Oh, I need that - can I try some?"

I dabbed a small amount under her eyes. "Cooling, isn't it?" I asked.

As I started to walk away Michele said, "Pam, let me see that product." I handed her the pen and she read out loud, "Skin perfecting pen - reduces spots, boils and pimples."

It was a good thing no one was paying attention but me. I know I turned three different shades of red. I gulped and thought, "Oh Lucy, what have you done!"

Michele smiled and handed it back to me. "Isn't that interesting. Good for under the eyes too, eh?"

I snatched the gel pen and zipped back to the skin care shipment to see what I had grabbed. Oh no! The boxes of gel pens were identical except for the front of the box where it showed a picture of a blue pen for under the eyes, and a green pen for blemish control. I immediately separated the boxes started praying that I hadn't messed up any one's eyes when Michele's client walked up. She wanted to buy one of the gel pens.

Thank heavens I was able to hand her the proper product - and thank heavens they contained all natural ingredients and were safe for all skin types. But I do wonder why Coyote makes these periodic visits to the salon!

Chapter Seven

HOT WAX STORY

I loved beauty school! Any time something new came out I was ready and willing to give it a try. Our instructors encouraged us to use family members to practice on. It was fun for my family at first, but later on they disappeared whenever I needed a guinea pig. I know it drove them crazy but I couldn't stand to miss out on anything new and exciting! All I required was a willing subject. I learned to take advantage of practicing new products and techniques on them because – as this story illustrates – even the simplest things never turn out like you anticipate.

I had a regular client who came for face waxing, and I noticed at the end of the process her cheeks were extremely red compared to the rest of her face. Even though I used the same wax I use for sensitive areas her cheeks always turned pink.

It reminded me of the first waxing I ever did, back in the early seventies. I was still in beauty school and back then waxing was not popular and we had very little call for it. However, I wanted to try it out and get some practice just in case a client asked for it, so I purchased a small container of depilatory wax to try.

We were invited to a New Year's Eve party so my husband at the time opted to try it. He was a furry guy. "So where do you want me to use it?" I asked.

"My cheeks," he said, because even though he shaved his face daily he didn't want to shave the hair on his cheeks and cause it to grow course and thick.

The directions that came with the wax suggested putting a candle under the wax to melt it. I didn't have a candle and decided to heat it up on the kitchen stove. I had no idea how hot the wax would get, but would soon understand why the directions said to use a candle!

I scooped up a small blob of wax with the wooden applicator and quickly applied it to his right cheek. He jerked when it hit his skin and yelled, "Ouch! That's hot!" Unfortunately his movement caused part of the wax to fall and drip on his sideburn (he wore an Elvis look at that time). "Hold still!" I shouted, "I have to spread the wax!"

I proceeded to his other cheek and even though I blew on the wax to cool it down, he winced and pulled away when it touched his skin. "That's really hot!"

"Will you just hold still?" I grumbled. I placed a small strip of cloth over the wax, held it tightly, and quickly ripped it off.

"Yow!!" he hollered. "Is it suppose to hurt this much?"

"I don't know!" I replied sharply. "I've never done this before. And remember, *you* were the one who asked for this."

After removing the wax his cheeks were bright red - if he'd had white hair he could have been Santa Clause! I put some cream on his face to calm and soothe the skin, and then recalled the wax that got onto his sideburn. I tried to remove the wax but there was no way – it was dry and hardened.

As a last resort I had to cut it out, leaving a small bald spot the size of a nickel within his dark thick sideburn. Now he had a dilemma: there was no way he was going to the party with a big hole in his sideburn.

"Not to worry," I said. Grabbing my black eyebrow pencil, I began filling in the space. "It will be dark at the party. I'm sure no one will notice." My husband was much more doubtful.

I was correct in that no one paid any attention to his sideburn during the party. However, everyone wanted to know where he went to cause his cheeks to get so sunburned. I just sipped my drink and innocently looked around the room as Mr. Macho glared at me.

As you can guess, it was a long time before I tried waxing again. I would have tried again sooner, but for some reason I couldn't find an obliging volunteer!

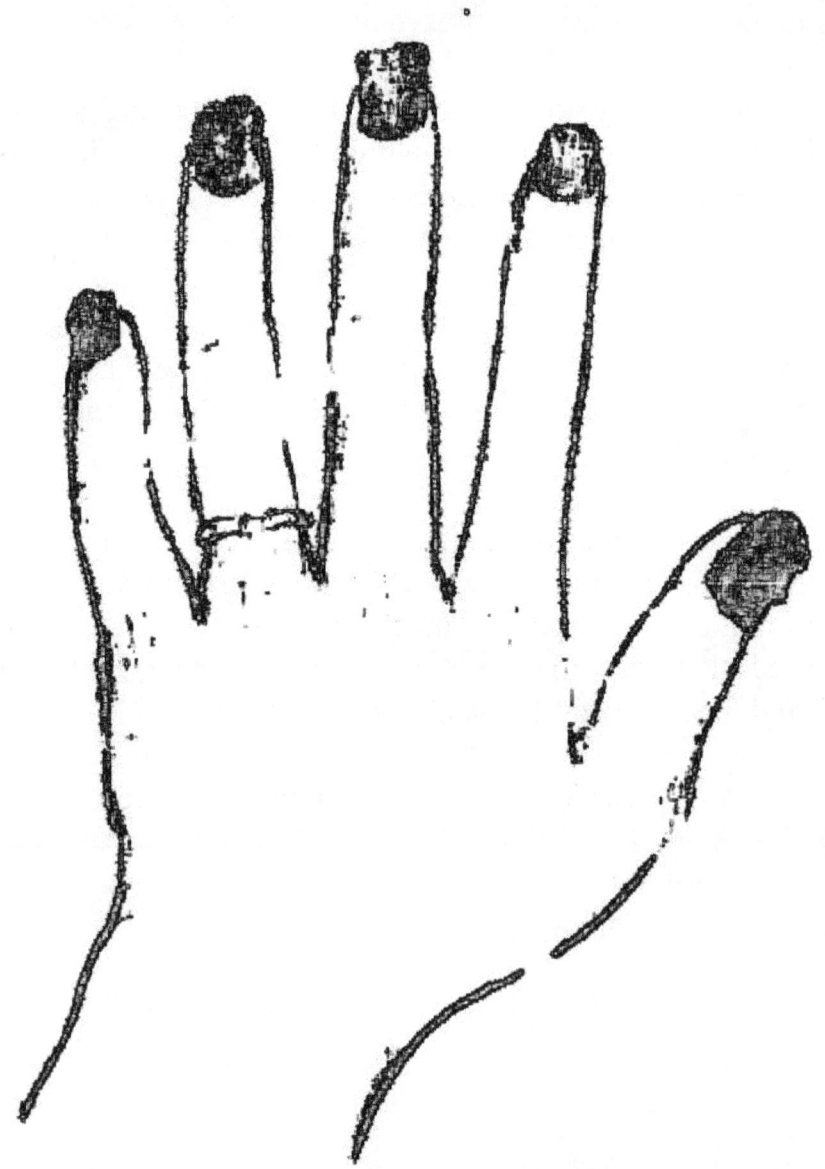

Chapter Eight

THE MANICURIST

It was never easy writing a newspaper column. The Commercial Appeal had tight deadlines so to stay ahead I combed the salon for any great experiences to share. Most were about clients. Rarely did anyone tell me a funny story about their own learning experiences. No matter how good we think we are, though, we all run into trouble at some point in our career. Once the client leaves your mind reels. You feel completely drained and upset by something you never meant to happen. The sad part is the client usually feels the same way.

Jolanda, our new manicurist, was having a difficult time repairing a broken nail on a client. I could see the frustration in her face as she struggled to get it just right. Finally she took the acrylic off she had been laboring over and started over again. It worked the second time and the client left happy. I had been watching her work at perfecting the nail for a long time.

"You okay?" I asked. I knew what it was like when things are not cooperating and you're trying to remain cool, confident and professional.

She looked up at me and smiled, seeing that I had been observing. "Yes, I'm just fine. Girl, you don't think I would really stress over that puny nail?"

"Oh no," I laughed, "not you Jolanda. I knew you had it under control."

She settled back in her chair and a big grin spread over her face. "There was a time in Beauty School when they gave me a client that wanted a full set of acrylic nails; now *that* was my worst nightmare." I knew I was in for a good story so I grabbed a chair.

Jolanda said the senior students were booked that day and the teacher decided it was time to put her on the floor. She was bored from practicing on clothespins for weeks and knew she was ready for the real thing. (Until you become proficient with the process, beauty schools have you use clothespins to practice forming acrylic nails on - but it's nothing like working on the real thing.)

"My client explained that the acrylic nails were not really in her budget, but all the women at work had them and tonight was their annual office party. She just had to have a set of her own. Thank God, she was a nice lady. I put on my most professional demeanor and began applying the nails. They kept getting bigger and wider. I spent an hour concentrating on them, but by the time I finally got them applied they were all thick and lumpy! Not a single nail turned out even. I looked up and saw her eyes bugging-out at the mess I had made, and after that I kept my eyes glued to the nails. I held tightly on to her hand because I was afraid she would try to make a run for it!

"I told her not to worry, that I would file them down and make them nice and even. Well, she kept looking at her watch so I glanced up at the clock over the reception desk. My Lord! I'd been working on her for two hours! I could feel the sweat rolling down my armpits and knew my deodorant couldn't take the strain.

"My regular nail file wasn't making a dent in the nails, so one of the students lent me her electric file. Girl, I worked on those nails till that file started smoking! By this time sweat was dripping in my eyes; but I was determined the nails were going to be perfect.

"My poor client had finally given up trying to get away. She leaned forward and laid her head on her arm in exhaustion. I'm thinkin' if this is what it takes to put on a set of nails, the salon I work in will need lounge chairs! 'I have to get back to work,' she said in a defeated voice. 'Just go ahead and put the polish on, maybe it will make them look better.'

"I tried talking her into a dark mocha polish in the hope it wouldn't call attention them, but instead she opened her purse and whipped out this wild neon-orange polish she had bought to match her outfit. By the time she left I had spent over three hours foolin' with those nails of hers; which still looked horrible - like big wads of chewing gum! I knew I was whipped."

Jolanda had me laughing so hard my sides were hurting. I asked her if the lady ever came back.

"No! Thank goodness! But because she was so patient with me I did call her the next day to see how her nails were. She laughed and told me she went right home and soaked them off before the party. I was glad because they looked awful, and I didn't want her telling anybody where she had them done!"

"*This young lady has delusions of Adequacy.*" EPRS S206

Chapter Nine

SOMETHING FOR NOTHING?

Not everyone who comes into your life leaves a lasting impression, but there are certain people you connect to instantly. It's as if the universe brought you together. Aussie was one of those people. We became fast friends after meeting at the apartment complex where we lived in. My place was three doors down from hers and we spent lots of time together. As relative newcomers to Los Angeles, we also experienced many wild and crazy things together. Sadly we lost touch after she moved back to Australia to be with her family. I moved back to Tennessee a year after that. But she left me with many wonderful memories that will never be forgotten.

When will we learn that you can't get something for nothing? In the early 80's I lived in Los Angeles in a small apartment complex near Santa Monica beach. I had a wonderfully funny neighbor from Australia named Gisella - we all called her Aussie. She had been working in the US for two years, earning money and sending most of it home. Her dad was investing the money to help her create a nest egg for when she decided to move back to Sidney. Her Australian-German family raised her to be thrifty, and in her desire to save Aussie cut corners anyway she could. She really knew how to squeeze a nickel!

She rode the busses in LA until she was able to find a car she could afford. One day Aussie came home with an old wreck she had paid five hundred dollars for – and it looked like it! Most of the paint was stripped and its body had lots of dents, but it ran. She found a place where she could get it painted for one hundred dollars, but they didn't offer many color choices. Unfortunately the car came out a dark, dull brown – almost the color of mud. They told her that waxing it would really make it shine. It most certainly did not.

However, Aussie was thrilled with her car deal and ecstatic about having wheels. The seat covers were stained and worn, and I tried to get her to spend twenty dollars for some new ones, but no way. Aussie had some lavender flannel material she had picked up for a song at a yard sale, and even though she had never sewn before, she borrowed a sewing machine and made her car a set of seat covers. To say they looked homemade was an understatement. It didn't matter to Aussie, though, because they worked and they were cheap.

One day she called me and said excitedly that she might get a new couch for free. One of her favorite lady regulars at the bar was giving the couch to Goodwill, but Aussie asked her to please let her have a "lookie-loo" in case she might want it instead (I loved her lingo).

"Great," I said. "Maybe you'll have it by the time I get home from work." This is where the story gets interesting.

After leaving work, Aussie drove to her friend's to check out the couch. Just as she pulled up to the curb two big bruisers carried the couch out of the house. She jumped out of her car to get a better look at the couch as the men continued carrying it to the sidewalk.

"Lady, are you the one that's come for this couch?" scowled one of the men, a biker with tattoos covering both of his massive arms.

The couch was completely worn out and had a big hole in the back with stuffing sticking out. "No, love, I've changed my mind. I don't want it," she said and got back into her car.

Not missing a stride, the men stepped over to her car and heaved the couch up on its roof where it teetered precariously.

"What the bloody hell?" Aussie exclaimed as she got back out of her car. "You can't do that!"

"Too bad, lady, we can't leave it out here. City ordinance says we can't leave furniture next to the curb. You just got yourself a couch."

The men did an about-face and quickly disappeared back into the house.

Poor Aussie! Since there was no way to get the couch off of her car there was nothing left to do but try and get it home. She carefully pulled out onto the street, and crept along. Terrified that the couch would slide off into oncoming traffic, she eventually reached a service station.

The attendant came out and surveyed the scene. "Hey lady, do you know you have a couch on your car?"

Frustrated and stressed out, Aussie asked if he could help lift it off.

"No way, lady, I've got a bad back. I can't lift that off your car."

Having no choice, Aussie inched her way back onto the boulevard. By now she was praying the police wouldn't see her and give her a ticket. Each time she came to a stop she held her breath as the enormous object teetered ominously back and forth. Other drivers honked their horns and screamed profanities as they tried to pass the "nut with a couch balanced on her car!" After what seemed like forever she finally made it back to her house.

At last, two neighbors helped her get the couch off her car and dumped it in the alley for the trash pick-up. When I arrived later she was still reeling from the ordeal. I sat cross-legged on the floor as she recounted her story, and rocked back and forth with laughter. She promised to stay away from free couches for a while - unless they are delivered!

***"If you aren't living on the edge … your taking up too much space.* Howard King**

Chapter Ten

SPRAY TANNING

At the beginning of summer we have people calling everyday to get a spray tan before going to the beach. A spray tan helps cover up the winter whiteness of the skin and gives one a healthy glow. Besides that, it gives the illusion of looking thinner, which definitely makes us feel better about ourselves. But buyer, beware - spray tans are applied in many different ways, some more complicated than others!

My daughter Wendy and I talk on the phone almost daily. With her living in Seattle and me in Memphis it's how we stay close and she keeps me up-to-date about her husband Robert and my grandsons, Dylan and Chris.

Recently I called and asked if she had time to talk. "Sure Mom, I'm just giving myself a pedicure. I'm finally able to get off the last of the orange stain from the spray tan I had last summer."

"I can't believe that color is still on your nails!" I said, and we had another good laugh about the incident. It was the first – and last – time she tried a spray tan.

Wendy and the family were going on a vacation, and she had not had time to get some color on her pale, winter skin. I vividly recalled our conversation on the phone.
"Mom," she said, "I have to tell you about my Heckawe experience yesterday (Heckawe is our word for "Where-the-heck-are-we"). I was reading the Sunday paper when I

saw an advertisement for spray tanning – enjoy a golden tan in minutes and look like you just got back from the Bahamas. Sweet! I thought. Sounds great and I don't have to use a tanning bed!

I made an appointment for the following day. Chris (who was 9 at the time) was curious about how it all worked and wanted to come with me. We were immediately ushered into a room called the tanning booth - basically a stall hung with big blue shower curtains around it. As I looked around for instructions, a woman appeared and started spouting off a list of directions at a hundred miles-a-minute.

I figured, how difficult could it be? But the lady kept adding more and more things, and it was getting very complicated. I began to worry that I wouldn't remember all the details!

Her instructions went something like this: make sure to keep your eyes closed when the spray starts; stand a certain way to ensure the best coverage on your legs; and your arms have to be held at a certain angle. The stance resembled that of a sumo wrestler.

She kept stressing how important it was to towel dry quickly after the spray stopped. The dye accumulates on the lower parts of the body, and if you don't quickly wipe it off your legs and feet will be a lot darker than the rest of your body.

"Finally she helped me in a shower cap that had to be put on perfectly with the ears outside and positioned just at the hairline. "We don't want a white band around the face," she chirped. Oh boy, I thought, that would really look great if that occurred!

Then she gasped, noticing that I wasn't wearing any nail polish on my hands or feet. Apparently this was a big deal because the nails would get discolored. She gave me something that looked and felt like Vaseline to put over them, and told me to make sure I completely covered the nails but not to get any on the skin or 'you could end up with white rings around your toes.'

And if all that was not enough to remember, she said to make sure my hands were turned the right way so that my palms wouldn't be sprayed.

Still running through the directions in my head, I got myself prepped and was finally ready for the spray tan. I stepped into the booth and closed the curtain. It was cool inside and I was shivering a bit. In front of me was a big blue button. I readied my position, took the correct stance, made sure my hands were turned the right way, pushed the button, and closed my eyes…but nothing happened!

Naked, cold, and afraid to open my eyes, I called to Chris, who was patiently waiting on the other side of the curtain, to go and find the lady and bring her back to see if there was a problem.

Just as the words left my mouth a fine, cold spray hit me all over. I screamed and jumped at least a foot in the air. It felt like being sandblasted with ice water!

"Chris asked if I was okay. I could hear worry in his voice, but was unable to speak because the spray would get in my mouth. So I held my breath and kept my mouth clamped shut until the spray finally stopped. I gasped for breath and quickly turned around to get my backside sprayed.

"I yelled out that I was fine just as the spray started up again, almost forgetting to turn my palms the other way.

"As soon as it stopped, I asked Chris to hand me a towel and began frantically wiping my legs, afraid I would end up with uneven color. As I stepped out of the stall, I remembered I needed to wipe the bottoms of my feet, so I hopped around trying to make sure the soles of my feet remained pink.

"What an ordeal! Despite efforts to protect my nails they were stained orange and would not disappear until they grew out. After that I decided that lying in a tanning bed doesn't seem like such a bad idea after all."

As I have said before, there are always two choices to make or two paths to take. One is easier - but that is its only reward.

Chapter Eleven

SNOBELLE'S BIRD

When will we learn not to interfere with nature's course? All we can do is to postpone the inevitable. At times it really is necessary to just move out of the way and let life go on.

At 2:30 a.m. I heard my cat, Snobelle, come through the cat door installed in my upstairs bedroom window. I heard a strange screech and sat straight up to switch on the lamp. Snobelle was on the floor, crouching over something.

Groan! Not another surprise! It was not the first time she brought a critter inside in the middle of the night.

Still groggy, I crawled out of bed and tiptoed over to see what she had. It was a baby bird and it was still alive! I got a tissue and carefully picked the bird up then carried it downstairs. I hated every time Snobelle brought something inside in the middle of the night. However, I was so sleepy I didn't want to bother with it, so I walked outside and carefully laid the bird on top of the trashcan. Praying Snobelle wouldn't find the bird, I stumbled back upstairs and went back to sleep, figuring I would deal with it in the morning if it was still there.

The next morning I went downstairs for coffee when my roommate David informs me he has found a live baby-bird under his truck.

"Yeah," I said, "Snowbell brought it inside last night. I put it on top of the trashcan."

"Why did you do that?" he asked.

"It was the middle of the night and I could hardly open my eyes," I grumbled, still feeling deprived of sleep from the ordeal.

David started lecturing me that I should have put the bird in a box and given it food, just like he had done after discovering it.

"David," I huffed, "it was two-thirty in the morning! Besides, I would have had to stay awake the rest of the night to keep Snobelle away from it!"

"Well, I don't have the heart to abandon any live creature," he said self-righteously. "I'll find a place to take it."

"Alright," I said warily. "You might want to try the Lictherman Center - it's an animal sanctuary not far from here."

"Well," he said, "I have to get the bird away from here. I think I'll take it over to Mom and Dad's house. They have plenty of woods and no cats around."

"Good idea," I replied as I watched Snobelle stand on her hind legs, trying to get a better view from the window of the bird inside the box.

Not long after that David returned looking disgruntled and still carrying the bird with him. "Can you believe Mom and Dad wouldn't take care of it?" he said in disbelief. "They said they had too many things to do and baby-sitting a bird wasn't one of them. They seemed shocked that I even asked them!"

"David," I explained, "baby birds have to be fed every hour to keep them alive. Years ago my children found a nest of three baby birds that had fallen out of a tree. We tried our best to save them, but within a week they all died."

I was thankful to be leaving for work because I knew David's obsessing over that bird would get on my every last nerve. Later in the day I told the story to Kathy, our receptionist. She told me of an animal rescue center in Cordova and gave me the number. I called David and passed along the information, hoping he would get help for the baby bird. But no such luck.

After arriving home I stepped onto the patio and saw the bird, still in its box. Snobelle was stretched out on the step, trying to pretend she wasn't interested in it, but every time it chirped I saw her ear twitch.

I went inside to find a very stressed-out David pacing the floor and running his fingers through his hair so much it stuck straight up as if he was wired. He saw me and said matter-of-factly "It looks like you're going to have to take care of the bird because I'm going back out on the road tomorrow."

"Oh no I'm not!" I nearly shouted. "You're not going to put that bird off on me! <u>You</u> decided to save it, now <u>you</u> decide what to do with it!"

"Fine! I'll find someone else to feed the bird," he said, doing his best to make me feel guilty. "How about Annie?"

I knew why he wanted to ask my best friend, Annie. With her big heart she couldn't say no to anyone.

Mortified, I replied, "There is no way Annie has time to care for a wild bird! Besides, she's out of town with her family." I smugly turned away and headed upstairs, hoping he would get the message that the bird was <u>his</u> problem.

"Well, what about your friend Jim? I know he lives out in the country," he called after me. I could feel my shoulders drawing up to my ears.

David knew my good friend Jim was coming by to take me out to dinner that evening. Feeling totally exasperated by this time I answered, "David, Jim is not going to take that bird home, so don't try to palm it off on him. Why don't you ask one of your friends?"

It wasn't until much later that night while rummaging through the fridge that I overheard David having a serious conversation with Snobelle. He told her that since she had captured the bird it rightfully belonged to her, so he was giving it back. She was going to have to figure out what to do with it (actually, Snobelle knew exactly what she was going to do with it). David was washing his hands of it.

51

Next morning the bird was gone. If he had let nature take its course we would have been spared from all of the drama. We all have rescuing tendencies, but more often than not the rescuer ends up becoming another victim! However, I did go to the pet store and bought a collar with a bell on it so Snobelle couldn't sneak up on any more critters. She had created more than enough drama already!

Chapter Twelve

A BROW WAX FOR CHRISTMAS

More and more men are coming to the spa for services, but nothing like the amount of women who come. Perhaps they feel that a shave and a splash of aftershave is plenty, but others are seeking out more specific grooming. After all, we all could use the extra help at times, plus it's a wonderful way to relax and feel pampered. Just getting a brow wax can make you feel like you've had an eye lift without plastic surgery!

Tuie was a new client who came to see me for an eyebrow and bikini wax. She had moved to Memphis and had been in the area for less than a year. "I usually wax and tweeze my own eyebrows," she said, "but I botched them up trying to tweeze them in the car while on a trip with my husband."

"Not to worry. I can fix them," I said.

I quickly cleaned up her brows and started waxing her bikini area. After a few minutes she smiled and said she was happy she found me. Her first bikini waxing in Memphis wasn't pleasant at all. She had been pregnant and her skin bruised afterwards. She believed the person was not experienced. Tuie asked if men ever came in the salon for facials.

"Yes, sometimes, but mostly they come for waxing."

She started laughing and recounted the time she waxed her husband's "unibrow." He had no idea what she was going to do when she walked up to him, applied a small amount of wax between his eyebrows, and quickly yanked it off with a cloth strip. Taken completely by surprise, he screamed and jumped back. "Honey! What did you do that for?!" he cried. It brought tears to his eyes.

She confided that she had secretly wanted to do it ever since they got married. "I did apologize to him. But now he'll never let me do it again," she grumbled. "If I can get my bikini area waxed surely he can handle a little brow waxing!"

"He's just such a macho man. I've tried to get him to go to a professional and have it done, but no way. Jack was born and raised in a small town in Mississippi and flat refuses to go in to a 'girlie place.' Said he wouldn't be caught dead in a spa."

"Men do come into the boutique to buy things for their wives," I offered. "Just explain to him that we have a private room upstairs and I can get him in and out in a flash."

"Well, I can try," she said doubtfully. "Maybe I can get him to come in and buy me a gift certificate for Christmas."

Before she left Tuie prepaid for her husband's brow wax and set up an appointment. "The earlier the better," she said. "When he gets here just tell him it's already paid for and you will wax his unibrow."

"Oh no!" I said, "You have to tell him ahead of time. Tell him I'm good at waxing and won't hurt him." She smiled and waved as she went out the door. "Good luck!" I said, wondering if he would actually show up.

One of my next clients decided to get a facial with her brow wax. I checked my book and saw I had time, mainly because I had forgotten about Jack. I'll be danged if he didn't show up right at one o'clock.

I needed fifteen more minutes to finish the facial, but found a stopping point when the mask I had applied wasn't quite ready to take off. I didn't have a second room, but figured I could take Jim to another section of the boutique area and wax his brow. Besides, it would only take a minute.

As luck would have it, several women were milling around in the boutique, looking at items and checking out sale prices. I had no choice but to give them the stink eye and hoping they would leave so I could bring him upstairs.

But by the time they finally left Jim had been waiting fifteen more minutes! I flew down the stairs to find him pacing in front of the door and talking on his cell phone. I could tell he was nervous and could bolt at any second if he had to wait longer.

I explained my room predicament and assured him that I could still do his wax and that we would not be disturbed. I then said a silent prayer.

I showed him upstairs and led him to a chair. He leaned his head back so I could apply the wax. Then he started laughing. "Yeah, when Tuie did this to me I thought she was going to kiss me. I had no idea she was going to wax my brow," he said.

"Just relax," I said, "This might sting a bit." I zipped off the wax and heard a loud yelp. "Is there blood?" he winced. "I want some blood dripping down my face."

"Sorry," I said, "No blood, but it is kind of red. Would you like some concealer on your skin?"

"No, I want her to know I suffered."

That evening I found out that he did indeed buy his wife a hundred dollar gift card, even after all that torture. Ah yes, a man after my own heart.

Chapter Thirteen

EDSEL'S EYEBROWS

Many of my problems originate from the business I'm in - it's called people pleasing. I feel best knowing that I have helped a friend, or that I have brightened someone's day. I love seeing my clients happy and smiling at the end of their appointments. I want this for all of my clients. Sometimes everything backfires even though you have only the best intentions at heart. My only explanation for this is that people have a hard time with change, me included. Later on we get used to a new look or style and like it better. Well, most of the time.

"Pam your client is here," they called over the intercom. Although my main work is in esthetics, I generally have hair clients as well. It was Edsel's second appointment with me and it had been quiet sometime since I saw him and his wife Barbara.

Edsel and I go way back to my childhood when we lived in the same small town in east Tennessee. He and my oldest brother Lee became best friends in junior high, and like most of Lee's close friends he hung out at our house on a regular basis. Lee and Edsel were a lot alike, always cracking jokes and making fun of everything. They always had us laughing about their antics in and out of school. Edsel loved our family and we did him.

The first time he came in for a haircut I was reminded that we had known each other for over 50 years! "Yikes!" I said, "Don't tell anyone here! They all think I'm younger." Thank you, God, for make-up and good skin care.

When I saw Edsel this time he was sitting across from the reception desk, looking much older and smaller than I remembered. It looked like he had shrunk! He was not his vibrant self.

He came upstairs to my station and took the baseball cap off his head. He had lost most of his hair on top and the rest was solid white. He appeared washed out and tired to me.

"Are you okay?" I asked.

"Well, I have been under the weather, but I'm feeling better today. Just need my monthly grooming."

Edsel loved coming to the day spa ever since his barber had retired. That's when Edsel called me to see if I was still in the hair business. I loved our visits because we laughed and joked about old times whenever he came. I gave him a nice, relaxing shampoo, quickly draped him, and spun him around to face the mirror. Picking up my scissors and comb I started trimming his hair. I was on a mission to make my friend look and feel younger!

I had told my brother Lee that Edsel was coming to me for haircuts now, and Lee told me a funny joke about hair. I shared it with Edsel and the laughter brought color back to his cheeks. By the time I finished his haircut he was starting to look more like his old self.

"Pam, can you get rid of all this hair around my ears? I don't know why the older I get hair grows everywhere except where I need it to!" he said as he fingered the few remaining strands on top of his head.

"I can use the clippers, but it is really temporary. Have you ever used wax to take off the hair?" He shook his head no. "Come upstairs to my esthetician room and I'll quickly take care of it."

He laid down on my table and I gingerly spread the wax around the fuzzy place. This particular wax was a hard wax to be used on tender areas. After the wax becomes hard it is easy to remove with little or no pain - well maybe a little sting. As I finished I explained it would be several weeks before the hair would show up again. He loved it! I also noticed his eyebrows were long and needed trimming. They looked a mess!

"Edsel let me wax your eyebrows just to clean them up a little."

"Sure, whatever you think I need," he replied.

I studied his face and said, "What you need is some expression. Your eyebrows are the same, solid white as your hair. Let me tint your eyebrows, you'll love it!" I assured him.

"Well, if you think it will help, go for it!" he said.

I mixed up a light brown tint and added a 4% volume developer and applied the color with a small brush. Sometimes color will work within minutes, but grey hair can be resistant and take longer. I had to get some water to remove the color and by the time I returned the color had gone dark after only a couple of minutes! Oops! I hate when this happens!

I cleaned off the color immediately started applying color remover, but it didn't help. Edsel's eyebrows were still dark – Groucho Marx dark! Well here goes nothing I said to myself as I handed him the mirror.

"Wow! I don't remember my eyebrows being that dark."

"Not to worry," I said, "the color fades quickly in a few days. It might take a little getting used to. They have been white for a long time. Here, try these on." I handed him his glasses and he put them on. "That's better! They hardly show."

Fortunately Edsel was a good sport and open to change. "They look great!" he grinned. He went on his way and I continued on to my next client. Several hours passed and then my cell phone rang. It was Barbara, Edsel's wife.

"Pam," she yelled, "What have you done to my husband?!" She was very upset.

"What's wrong?" I asked.

"He just doesn't look like himself!" she said.

I happened to think he looked better. I also wondered why <u>he</u> didn't call if he had an issue. Well look whose henpecked. "I was under the impression he was okay with the color."

"Well, I'm not!" she shouted.

"Barbara, it's not permanent," I tried to explain, but she wasn't hearing any of it. "I'm free in the morning. I'll drop by and bring a stronger color remover. Trust me. I can get most of the color off. In the meantime put some Vaseline on his eyebrows tonight. That will help."

"I just can't believe you did that to him!" she said with disgust. "Did you also wax his eyebrows?"

"Um, no," I fibbed. "I just trimmed them."

"Whatever. I'll call you tomorrow," she grumbled and hung up the phone.

By now I was in shock. I never thought Barbara would get so tore up over this. It really bothers me when a client is not happy with my work, but to have a good friend be upset threw me for a loop.

That evening I tried to quiet my mind and meditate, but all I could think of was Barbara yelling, "What did you do to my husband?!" Harrumph! I knew him way before she did! He was always like a big brother to me. Why wouldn't she let me talk to him? Did it really change his looks that drastically? He even had a spring in his step when I finished with him! Perhaps he looked younger than she did now and she was jealous. She caught me off guard. I wanted to explain to her that I saw Edsel with no expression. Jay Leno and David Letterman both have white hair and really dark eyebrows that they probably tint. I wanted her to understand why I did it, and that grey hair usually takes a long time to turn darker but Edsel had some weird chemical reaction to the color!

At the end of my meditation I noticed I had a missed call and a phone message. It was from Barbara! Arrrrgh! I didn't want to listen to the message and decided I would deal with it in the morning.

However, I hardly slept a wink. I was not looking forward to hearing Barbara's wrath on my phone. I finally listened to her message before heading off to work.

"Hey Pam, its Barbara," she said on the message. "Don't bother coming by tomorrow. Edsel's enjoying all the attention from our friends that we met for dinner tonight. It seems everyone's trying to figure out what's different about him. They can't put their finger on it and he's certainly not going to tell. Boy, he had them all stirred up!" she laughed. It seems that he adored being the center of attention.

The next week I shared the story with my meditation group. They were holding their sides and wiping tears from their eyes as I finished the story. "Why did you tell her to put Vaseline on his eyebrows?" one of them asked. "Does that really work?" "No!" I grinned, "But it was worth a try to get her off my back!"

"We can go through an experience or we can grow through an experience." **Unknown**

Chapter Fourteen

THE BRAZILIAN

I have talked many clients through their first Brazilian waxing. I was confident in putting them at ease and having them relaxed and comfortable by the time I began. Some clients have stopped me halfway through the process, telling me it was all they could handle. However, this was the first time I spent most of the appointment trying to get them to undress!

I was walking downstairs at the Spa when I heard Susan, its owner, explaining the benefits of a Brazilian bikini wax to Margie, one of her regular clients. Susan was giving her a manicure and as she described the extent of the true Brazilian Margie's eyes grew as big as saucers. Susan shared the first time she took it all off and told her what a great experience it was for her.

"I definitely want to try something different," said Margie. "Maybe I'll have my bikini line waxed."

"No!" Susan said. "Take it all off. You'll love it."

"You think I should?" Margie said as she bit her lower lip. "Doesn't it hurt?"

"Well, that all depends." Susan lowered her eyes and whispered, "Everyone's different but you could handle it, I'm sure. And you will love our esthetician Pam. She's great and has lots of experience. Go for it!"

"Do you think it will make me feel sexy?" Margie whispered?

"I guarantee it," said Susan.

She checked my book and made her an appointment later that afternoon. Margie found me before she left and asked if she could change her mind and just wax her bikini line. "I'll do whatever you want," I assured her.

When she returned to the salon later she looked flushed. "Well, Margie, are you ready to do this?"

"I think so. I've never done this before, so you'll have to tell me what to do."

"Generally you need to take off your clothes, including your underwear, and hop up onto the table."

She quietly disrobed and climbed onto my table. "Honey," I said, "this really does work better if you remove your underwear."

Maggie laughed nervously. "I can't believe women really do this! I mean, it seems so weird."

"You'd be surprised how many women get the Brazilian. It's very popular."

"How long have you been doing them?"

"For at least five years now."

"Five years! Are you kidding me? Where have I been? I thought they came out about a year ago." Margie squirmed on the table trying to decide if she really wanted to go through with this.

"Maggie," I laughed, "you can change your mind. Perhaps you aren't ready. It really isn't a big deal. Just go for the bikini line wax. You can try the Brazilian another time." But Margie was obstinate.

"No, I can do this!" she said. "I've been psyching myself up all afternoon. I want to go for it!"

I waited for a moment or two. "You still need to remove your panties for me to do this." I was growing exasperated by her unwillingness to disrobe.

"Okay. I'm going to do it," she said, and finally disrobed, for a married woman with children I was amazed at her modesty.

"Why don't we clean up your bikini line, and if you want me to take more off, just let me know." When I pulled off the first wax strip Margie shot up in a sitting position.

"Yow! That hurts!" she yelped.

"You'll have to get used to it. Remember, we can stop at any time."

Margie laid right back down. "Keep going, Susan told me to drink a beer. I should have had two. And now that I think about it, three shots of tequila might also do the trick."

I turned up the stereo and told her to relax and breath, kind of like Lamaze,

"Oh my god! #*#*!!," she gasped after the next wax strip. "It's like having a baby! Do many women really ask for this?"

"Remember to breathe and relax. Tell me something about yourself." I was hoping to take her mind off the process as I finally reduced her bikini line down. I asked Margie if she wanted to take a look and tell me if she wanted any more taken off.

"No thank you," she said. "I'm not going to look at it until I go home."

I cracked up! "Are you kidding me?"

"No. I don't want to look at it till later."

I knew I had seen everything then. "Do you want me to continue?" I asked.

"How much is left?"

"Not much. I think you'll like your new look," I smiled.

Margie unclenched her hands. "Okay, let's have this baby!" she laughed. "I can't believe I'm doing this!" she said giddily for the tenth time.

I figured it was a rite of passage for her, the first bikini wax of her adult life. I thought this much better than a tattoo or a piercing. With the help of my Angels I quickly finished the task at hand. I cleaned off the skin and applied a soothing antiseptic crème to take away the sting.

"You can open your eyes now. I'm finished. Are you sure you don't want to take a look?"

Margie shook her head no.

"I'm proud of you," I said. "That was big for you to take on if you never have been waxed before."

"I'm glad I did it," she smiled. "But don't tell Susan. She didn't think I would!"

At that moment I was convinced that Susan could sell ice cream to Eskimos!

Chapter Fifteen

LAUGHING COYOTE STORY

While finishing the final edit of this book I came across a story I had written about my older brother Lee. He was a master story-teller and the entertainer of the family. Famous for his jokes and stories, Lee would tell them in a manner that had you believing everything was true – right up to the punch line. He left a lasting impression on everyone he met. Eldon, or Lee, as most knew him, made his transition on August 31, 2012. He was greatly loved by many and will be sorely missed.

I love visiting with my brother Lee in Los Angeles. Lee (Laughing Coyote) always had a funny joke or story to tell. He told me he really enjoyed reading my Angel Karma stories and recounted one of his own that occurred many years ago at Mother's hair salon. He had me laughing before he even started telling it.

Our mother owned a beauty salon in the small town of Kingsport in the early fifties. Each Sunday Lee was responsible for cleaning it for the coming week. She gave him five dollars to wipe down all the mirrors and windows, sweep and mop the floor, and tidy everything up. Already the budding entrepreneur, Lee recruited a few of his buddies to do the work for him and treated them to a movie as payment. Since the Sunday matinee was only fifty cents back then, he got the work done with no personal effort and still pocketed a nice profit. Sweet!

One of the friends, Charlie, was a blond, fair-skinned lad who was forever broke and loved hanging around Lee because he always seemed to have money. From his standpoint Lee was practically rich. But Charlie was always trying to get something for nothing—and that annoyed Lee.

After they finished cleaning the salon one day, Charlie asked Lee if he knew how to dye hair. "Of course, my mother's a beautician!" he boasted. Charlie asked if Lee would dye his hair black and give him a trim. "Sure. Piece of cake," Lee said confidently, and went to the supply room for a bottle of jet-black hair dye.

He sat Charlie down at one of the stations and faced him away from the mirror. That way he couldn't see that Lee had no idea what he was doing. Back then, hair dye was very concentrated. It worked instantly when applied. Lee tried to remember how Mother colored her client's hair. Lee used a brush and started applying the dye, but as soon as he did it started running in rivulets down Charlie's forehead, cheeks, and neck. Lee grabbed a towel to wipe it off only to discover that the dye had already stained the skin dark purple! Lee tried desperately to wash it off, furiously scrubbing the skin and neck with shampoo, but it was futile.

After Lee dried Charlie off and removed the towel, the other guys slapped their hands over their mouths to keep from bursting out laughing. Lee was stressing. How could he remove the stains? He grabbed some Ajax cleanser and scrubbed Charlie's skin raw to try and lighten the purple streaks, but it did nothing. Charlie's hair was black, his scalp was purple, and dark purple lines ran down his face. Lee was very nervous.

"What's taking so long?" Charlie whined. "I thought you were going to give me a trim." Lee decided that might help it look better. With comb and scissors in hand, he started cutting his hair. It didn't take long before Lee realized it did not help! He asked one of his other friends to give it a try and see if they could get it to come out even. Unfortunately, poor Charlie's hair just got shorter and shorter until it looked like someone had placed a small bowl on his head and trimmed around it. At that point the guys could no longer hold back their fits of laughter and Charlie realized something was seriously wrong.

He finally looked in the mirror and could not believe his eyes! He started crying and lamenting that his mother was going to kill him! Lee tried to calm him down, telling him that the dye stains would come off in no time. Then he rummaged about for a knit cap and handed it to him. Charlie pulled it down over his ears and they headed on to the movies.

The following day Lee came to the salon. Without saying a word, Mother grabbed him and marched him out back. She gave him an intense "dressing down," describing how Charlie's mother had stormed into the salon that morning, ranting that Lee had ruined Charlie's hair. Years later we found out that Charlie had been with his mother. He stood behind her with his head hung low. When she yanked the knit cap off, Mother burst out laughing at the sight. She couldn't stop laughing even though Charlie's mother threatened to sue. She managed to remove the streaks from his face and neck with color remover, and told Charlie he would just have to let his hair grow out.

Charlie ended up missing two weeks of school and the next time he saw Lee he yelled fiercely at him, swearing that he could never let him near his hair again. Of course it didn't drive him away from the Sunday afternoon cleanings though. After all, it was for a free movie!

***"We start cutting our wisdom teeth the first time we bite off more than we can chew!"* Herb Caen**

Chapter Sixteen

"Looking for Hair Therapy"

The Beauty Business is at the top of the professions that can help people Feel better about themselves, it is a given when we like the way we look we naturally feel better.

Getting a fresh hair cut can definitely be a perk to ones self-esteem. A simple eyebrow wax can make you feel and look like you just had a Brow Lift. I hear this all the time from my clients. My Motto: Everyone can be improved on!

It seems when people find out I'm in the beauty business they want to tell me their disastrous "Hair Story." I met Betty Jean at a New Years Eve party. When I told her I was in the beauty profession she immediately went into her story, explaining how when she was in her early twenties she felt very insecure about herself and didn't like who she was very much. She hadn't been in a relationship for some time and was feeling like an ugly duckling.

She knew she had some difficulties with her self-esteem, but was unwilling to look at her problems in a deep way; instead, she fell into the trap of looking for outer solutions to get what she wanted. She said she shopped a lot, mostly for clothes and shoes, to make herself feel better, but it didn't help much. One day when she was really feeling lonely, she met a hairdresser who worked in a chic salon (which really impressed her) in an affluent area of East Memphis.

She thought he would know what was really cool! In no time she confided in him and complained about not having a boyfriend and wondering what she could do about it. Betty Jean said he leaned back, squinted his eyes, and scrutinized her from head to toe. He said he could help her, and convinced her that her prince would never show up unless she did something about her "frizzy, mousy-colored hair…and girl…those eyebrows…they have to go! She thought, "Oh Boy! This is my lucky day, getting to meet him!" Betty Jean wanted to believe that her appearance was indeed her only obstacle to love.

She made an appointment with him the next day. She was excited and full of expectations. How easy this would be, in by nine, out by two, loved by midnight…she was ready! She had her hair cut off, colored red, and permed. As he constantly assured her of how fantastic she looked, he plucked her eyebrows (as she described) to a single hairs-breath. To add insult to injury she had to pay $300 for the damage, and then cried all the way home. She said it took six months to recover from that mistake and to look like herself again. She never even got one date out of the deal… "If I were a guy I wouldn't have asked me out either. I looked like Little Orphan Annie." By now I was laughing my head off. Poor Betty jean, she would have been better off spending her money on a few therapy sessions.

Betty Jean learned a big lesson…Beauty Salons are for hair problems not heart problems…as…Angel Karma Strikes Again!

Chapter Seventeen

"The Italian Stallion"

It's amazing what people will try when they start losing hair. Our hair is our crowning glory, and not every man looks great with a shaved head.

An experienced Hairdresser can quickly recognize if a man is wearing a full toupee or a partial wig worn to cover a bald spot. If you are losing your hair and it really bothers you the best thing is to find a reputable company that has a reputation for making a natural looking hairpiece that fits the head and matches your hair color.

Derwin was a regular to the salon, in his late 30's and never married. He was a funny (peculiar) little guy and did not have much going for him except his thick sandy-blonde head of hair, which was his crowning glory. His hair was starting to thin and he was always worried about losing what he still had, complaining about how hard it was to find someone to date, and fearing his hair loss would keep him from ever finding the "one." When I shampooed his hair he endlessly cautioned how much, if any, hair was caught in the strainer (he was so paranoid). He confided to me that he even slept on a silk pillowcase in hopes that it would keep his hair from rubbing off in his sleep. "Derwin", I said, "are you really losing that much hair?"

A pained expression came on his face as he winced and tenderly patted his head…I saw I had touched a raw nerve. It seemed lately he had been losing more hair than usual. He had tried Rogain first, with no luck, and was now using Nioxin religiously. He was trying everything available. Someone had told him cayenne pepper would stimulate his scalp, "Yes," I laughed, "but only if you drink it." "Derwin, if it's not hereditary, it could be anything. How's your diet, do you have any thyroid problems? I've read a weak spleen affects the hair, or it might be hormonal, maybe high testosterone," I said. I then noticed the color drain out of his face.

I had forgotten what a hypochondriac he was. Now he was going to worry the stew out of me about his thinning hair. His hair obsession was getting out of hand as he ordered every new hair therapy he could find. He seemed to feel it was his duty to keep me informed of any new thinning hair products that he came across; wanting to know if he came for a hair cut could he bring pictures of styles that he thought would make his hair look fuller. He was becoming a neurotic pain – to say the least. I could set my watch by Derwin, he came like clockwork every three weeks, but it had been 6 weeks since he had been to the shop.

One day he showed up wearing a baseball hat and a 'you won't believe what I have done' look on his face. "Derwin, what are you doing with that hat on," I laughed, "I would think you might be afraid it would rub all the hair off your head!?" He sat in my chair and with a sheepish grin looked at me and said, "I got a perm." I was shocked! "Why did you go and do that?" I asked. "I'm sorry," he said. "It was a spur of the moment thing and I have regretted it ever since." "Who talked you into getting a perm!" I exclaimed, trying to picture Derwin with curly hair. "Now Pamie, I would have come in sooner, but I knew you were going to be mad at me." He had such a pained expression on his face; I could not be upset with him for long. "It all started in the health food store a few weeks ago," he began. "I went in to buy some vitamins, and this guy came up to me, thinking I worked there, and wanted to know what a good brand of vitamin C was. I couldn't take my eyes off of his hair, it was so thick and wavy, and before I knew it I blurted out what a great head of hair he had. He laughed and said, "Thanks it's a perm," and he proceeded to tell me where he had gotten it done, and how easy it was to take care of. He said just to tell his hairdresser 'Danny had sent me' and she would take good care of me.

I called the salon the next day and she said if I came in within the hour she could take me. I really didn't have time to think about it; I just dashed on over there. As soon as I said, "I want a perm like you gave Danny, "she raised an eyebrow and started to grin. "Most men who meet Danny want to look like him," she chortled. I should have known right then that this might not be a good idea. She ran her fingers through my hair and said a perm would make my hair look thicker. I was hooked. She then shoved a Men's Hair Styling book at me and said to pick out a picture of something I liked. I looked at all the pictures and finally found one picture of a good looking hunk with soft wavy dark-brown hair, "the Italian Stallion" look. I always wanted to look like that…but by the time she was finished with me, my hair looked more like and Afro-American.

I went right home and washed it a dozen times, it looked dry and frizzy. I went back to the stylist and she conditioned my hair, and sent me out with it wet, and a sack full of expensive products. Nothing she gave me helped, and that was when I started wearing a hat. By now I was laughing out loud, wiping tears from my eyes. "Let me see your hair," I said. He couldn't look at me as he slowly lifted off the hat, and his hair immediately exploded into a huge frizz-ball! I doubled over with laughter. Poor Derwin, he was far from the Italian Stallion…as Angel Karma Strikes Again!

Chapter Eighteen

"Too Natural For Me"

Our taste buds are developed when we are young and it starts when we are given baby food out of a jar. I give credit to my father for introducing new foods to me when I was young. In fact we were not allowed to leave the table until we had tried a new dish we had never had before. I remember crying, not wanting to taste something new when most times when I did, it tasted better than it looked or smelled.

In 1980 while living in Los Angeles I had my first introduction to Sushi (raw fish). This event came about with a good friend who knew what to order, everything I tried tasted good. I loved it all, well except for Sea Urchin, I never acquired a taste for it, and to me it smelled and tasted foul.

Tom Singin' Bear, a fellow Heckawe and good friend who knows I'm a health food advocate and into living a healthy life style, called me wanting to share his health eating experience with me. Tom comes from a small town in Mississippi and was raised on country cooking. He is a real meat and potatoes kind of guy. He proceeded to tell me about this 'crazy lady' that the company he worked for had hired to show them how to cook a healthy meal, and share the many benefits of changing their eating habits.

Because of the rising cost of health care (quoting his words) the company had hired this lady nutritionist to teach them how to eat. From the beginning Tom said the food looked suspicious, like nothing he had ever seen before. It looked awful and tasted worse. "The company told us the lady they hired had a Ph.D.," he laughed, you know "Piled Higher and Deeper."

Next to my brother, Tom is one of the funniest men I know, and he had me laughing my head off by the time he finished this story. Tom said, "The Nutritionist told us, before she got into cookin' healthy, she used to work for a catering company and was noted for making the best carrot cakes in town, but after many years of cookin' for a caterer, and going through a stressful divorce, she had put on a lot of extra weight and decided to change her bad eating habits. She had lost 75 lbs!" Continuing with his story, Tom said he tasted the healthy meal she prepared for them that day, and quickly decided she needed to go back to making carrot cakes.

"You know, 'if it ain't broke – don't fix it'. It didn't take me long to realize her efforts at cookin' health food was not her forte. It reminded me of that famous old saying, "Those that can – Do. Those that can't – Teach." Tom, what in the world did she cook for you?" I asked. "Now Pam, you know with a knife and fork nothing is safe around me. I'll try anything once but this was the yuckiest tasting mess I have ever put in my mouth. It would make a freight train take a dirt road," he said. "I know now why she's divorced, a man would be justified to whup his wife if she ever fixed him a meal like that." "Tom, you have yet to tell me what she prepared for you." I giggled. "It was some kind of a weird looking roll-up that was filled full of green things (looked like weeds) I took a big bite and bit into a pod of garlic, which brought burning tears to my eyes and took my breath away. Me and garlic don't mix – can't stand the stuff," he said.

"Well Pam," said Tom, "the more I chewed, the bigger it got. I was thinking, 'don't let me vomit', as I eyeballed the closest trash can. I must have looked like a rabid dog as I headed for it. I guess you could say, what I was eating did add color to my complexion – by then I had turned blue. I hurried past the company's in-house doctor, who stopped me, saying, "Now Tom, give it a chance, this food is good for you." I thought, what does he know about food? The guy's a vegetarian – he's never had any real food to eat. I'm trying to get to the restroom, and I look back and see most of the people in the room are following me. This healthy food had completely messed up my taste buds. I would have to deal with this stinky garlic breath all day, and I couldn't wash my hands enough to get rid of the smell either.

By the time I came out of the restroom she was mixing up this concoction of raw oatmeal, raisins, apples and nuts. Then she poured some kind of dark thick liquid over it. What on earth was it? And who would eat it? It looked like horse food to me-covered in shoe polish and sawdust. I'm not into eating raw oats; I don't care how healthy horses are. I decided I had tried enough, as I watched the three 'health nuts' in the group – you know – the kind that only weigh 98 pounds and live off of rice cakes and water. Oh, they were thrilled with what she had prepared. "Tell me your recipe," they gushed. It made me sick to listen to 'um.

They brought her in again a couple of weeks later to show us her healthy protein shake. I had smartened up by then and knew better this time. I would only taste after everyone else. I wanted to see who was left breathing. "What was in the shake," I asked, did you taste it?" "The shake consisted of soy and water, and a scoop of Juice Plus Vanilla Complete, strawberries and bananas, and some stinky smelling yeast." "Brewers yeast," I said. "Then she ground up some flaxseed and green tea leaves in a coffee grinder and put it in the blender, and as soon as I saw that, I knew she had ruined it," said Tom.

"Well what did it taste like?" I asked. "Like bananas mashed on the floor, with the consistency of cat litter mixed in milk," he said. By now we were both whooping and laughing as I pictured the look on his face after tasting the shake………as Angel Karma Strikes Again!

Chapter Nineteen

"A Shaky Situation"

How many times have we said why did I allow myself to get talked into this. They probably saw 'Sucker' written across my forehead when I walked through the door! What was I thinking, why did I volunteer for this, at the time it seemed like a good idea, something so simple could not possibly backfire on you!

"Wow, that was a great adjustment, Dr. Mike," I said to my chiropractor. I had been complaining to him about my lower back hurting, as my work involved leaning over my table for long periods of time.

"What is your work, Pam?" he asked. "I'm an esthetician, and I work in a salon and day spa," I said. "This past month I have been extremely busy seeing more clients for waxing and facials."

A big grin came over his face, as he said, "I had my eyebrows waxed once. Now that was an experience!" I was surprised when he told me, because I couldn't imagine he would even consider doing that. Dr. Mike was a big man. He needed a strong body to handle his practice, and you could tell he worked out on a regular basis. "So you only did it once. What happened?" I asked.

He started to laugh and said, "I was visiting my wife's family one Sunday. Her sister's best friend was there, and she was in beauty school at the time. She said she needed more practice, so she asked me if she could wax my eyebrows.

"Even though I would be her first male client, I didn't really see the harm in it. I had never had my eyebrows waxed before, but she assured me she was just going to clean them up and get rid of my unibrow. She said it would only take a few minutes! So I gave in."

"Did she have a table for you to lie on?" I asked. "I always have my clients lie down for a brow procedure, and I have a great magnifying light that shows every hair." "Well, no," Mike replied. "We were actually in the kitchen, and she just had me sit in a chair and hold my head back. But as she started toward my face, I noticed her hand was trembling. The closer she got to my face, the more her hand shook."

At this point in his story I was thinking, "*Hmmm... this is going to be interesting*." "Since I'd never had a wax before, you can imagine my surprise when she yanked the wax off!" He continued, "She then proceeded to wax the other eyebrow."

"Did it hurt?" I asked. "Yes it hurt!" he replied. "It brought tears to my eyes, but being the good sport that I am, I went through with it. When she finished, I raised my head and looked at my wife with pride. She immediately gasped when she saw me and stared wide-eyed at me.

"She had yelled, 'Oh no! Half your left eyebrow is missing!' and I reached up to touch the place where my eyebrow had been. She was right – it was gone!" Mike said., "The most amazing part is that the girl had never let on anything was amiss. She had a total poker face and didn't say a word."

"Unbelievable!" I said with a chuckle. "Maybe she thought if she didn't say anything you wouldn't notice half your eyebrow was missing."

"I don't know what she was thinking," he said, as he started to laugh as well. "She did give me an eyebrow pencil to fill in the spot, but I kept forgetting to use it. I tried to act like nothing was wrong, but my patients couldn't stop starring at me like, 'What happened to you?' I never let on – I was not going to explain myself to anyone! I just acted like nothing had happened.

"In the end, my wife and I decided that it doesn't matter whether you're a surgeon, dentist or esthetician, if you have a shaky hand, you need to get out of there!"

We roared with laughter together. What a hilarious story!

You might wonder what the Karma in the story is. Trust me there are no innocent bystanders, and no coincidences. When Dr. Mike being the nice obliging guy that he is, said he would help his sister's best friend by allowing her to get more practice he went in to rescue her and quickly became the victim. Think About It!

As Angel Karma Strikes Again

Summary

It is certain that many a truth is spoken in jest. It is also true that humor often hides the most important lessons we seek. And yes, laughter is incredibly healing. These principles helped guide me while writing "Angel Karma Strikes Again" – a collection of laugh-out-loud short stories about our human foibles.

These stories compile a myriad of hilarious true experiences from within the beauty business. Each story pertains to us on some level in that whatever we dwell on we will continue to attract. For in life there is no substitute for experience. It is only in our experiences we really learn and come to know life's important lessons. The question is how do we recognize them? We usually try to forget traumatic / embarrassing events by burying them deep inside our memory. Unfortunately we bury important life lessons along with them.

Thankfully, our angels are always nearby to remind us not to take it all so seriously. After all, we are born into this life to master lessons and gain wisdom. Some lessons are easier to learn than others, but if we take them all with a sense of humor they are ultimately easier to swallow. There is no question that they have benefitted me tremendously, and I hope they bring to mind experiences in the reader's life that they can relate to, and perhaps laugh at, themselves.

"Karmageddon; it's like, when everybody is sending off These really bad vibes, right? And then, like the Earth explodes and it's like, a serous bummer!

About the Author

Pam Drinnon is a native Tennessean. She was consciously awakened when she was only three years old, but it was after a powerful near death/angelic experience that she realized her mission in this life.

Pam is a professional healer, life and wellness coach, spiritual counselor and hypnotherapist. She practices and teaches Kinesiology 'The Power Reflex Method' a form of (muscle testing). This teaches one how to make **Conscious Contact** with your Sub-Conscious Mind and Super-Conscious Mind (Guardian Angel).

Pam is certified in the 'Emotion Code', a simple and powerful method of finding and releasing Trapped Emotions. The Sub-conscious mind will use Trapped Emotions to build a **Wall over the Heart**, creating a Heart Wall. Much of our unhappiness is due to negative trapped emotional energies within us.

Over the past '25 years' Pam has conducted workshops and seminars on connecting to your Angels and Guides, and Conscious Manifestation through the law of attraction.

Email: angelworks22@hotmail.com

Website: http://www.yourangelworks.com

$12.95

www.ingramcontent.com/pod-product-compliance
Lightning Source LLC
Chambersburg PA
CBHW051707040426
42446CB00008B/751